MW01232028

40 Days of
Renewal

A Journey Toward Freedom

Jeremy White
with Chris Lujan

Valley Church Press
Vacaville, California

Valley Church Press is a ministry of Valley Evangelical Free Church in Vacaville, California. This book was printed and produced via Createspace, an Amazon.com company for self-publishing.

Unless otherwise noted, all Scripture is taken from the New International Version (2011 ed.)

Valley Church is affiliated with the Evangelical Free Church of America (EFCA), a network of gospel-centered, autonomous churches working in partnership to bring the good news of Jesus Christ to every race, tribe, tongue and nation.

ISBN-13: 978-1519240699
ISBN-10: 1519240694

Printed in the United States of America

Createspace print date 12/1/2015

Acknowledgments

Writing a book (even a small book) is much more a team effort than one might think. We wish to thank the following people by name for their influence and contributions to the creation of this resource, realizing that we probably missed someone and we apologize in advance to whoever that is....

Thanks to the spiritual family at Valley Church, who walk this journey of grace and truth alongside of us. It is a joy to serve not only as spiritual leaders, but also fellow children of God alongside all of you!

Thanks to Judy Showalter for her willingness to review and edit the manuscript for us. Her volunteer investment was essential in producing a quality means of communication.

Thanks to Lori Shorter for her artistic gifts in designing the cover and for her willingness to share her skills so freely.

Thanks to our wives and families for their constant willingness to share us with others for the sake of God's kingdom. We want you to know that you are never second place and that you are, humanly speaking, at the top of the list of those for whom we exist.

Thanks, most importantly, to our Lord and Savior Jesus Christ who so selflessly serves us with His grace, patience, truth, and unconditional love. We hope and pray that He is glorified in this humble effort to set captives free.

How to Get the Most from This Experience

We're glad you picked up this book.

We wrote it because people like you are everywhere. People who love God, and yet struggle with feeling stuck in ways that cripple them with a constant sense of unrest.

We believe God created you awesomely and wonderfully (Psalm 139:14). Part of that wonder is that you were made with a body, soul and spirit (1 Thess. 5:23; Heb. 4:12).

Your body (Greek *soma*) is fairly easy to identify. It's the physical "tent" through which you perceive reality according to your five senses. What a beautiful gift the body is!

Your spirit (Greek *pneuma*) is your innermost being, your true essence or nature. It is the part of the Christian that exists in eternal union with God's Spirit and is perfected at the moment one trusts in Christ.

Your soul (Greek *psuche*) is your psychology or personality. It is the seat of your mind, will and emotions, and it is an indispensable part of who God created you to be.

Sometimes when we become Christians, we assume that the perfection of our spirit is the only transformation we need. We are united intimately and irreversibly with God, and we assume that our daily struggles will soon evaporate, or at least get much easier.

We understand and affirm that our spiritual union with Christ is an indispensable thing. It is the level at which we are constantly communing with our Creator, and it secures us with the gift of eternal life through that irreversible union.

However, when we become believers in Christ, we don't automatically wake up the next morning with new thoughts, feelings and behaviors. Many of our core beliefs took a long time to become rooted within us, and they will take some time to uproot and replace as well.

The Apostle Paul wrote that Christians can "be transformed by the renewing of (our) minds" (Rom. 12:2). In the realm of the soul, the mind is the place in which thoughts are conceived and beliefs are formed. The mind (thinking) has immeasurable influence upon our feelings (emotions) and ultimately our will (choices).

We believe that the foundational battle-ground for Christian growth is in the mind, which again, is part of the soul. The Greek word "transformed" is literally the word "metamorphosis" – the word we use to describe the process by which a caterpillar becomes a butterfly.

Think about that for a moment. The Bible claims that it is possible to experience a very real and radical process of transformation through the "renewing of our minds." One of the ways we renew our minds is by learning to identify false thinking and surrendering it to the truth found in Christ (2 Cor. 10:5).

Think for a moment about how powerfully your thoughts affect the way you feel. Imagine you are in a dark theater watching a scary movie. Everything from shadows and camera angles to music and sound effects are arrayed in such a way as to trick your mind into believing that danger is lurking.

In your rational thoughts, you know perfectly well that you are safe and sound in the theater with no real danger to fret about. Yet, as you set your thoughts on the sights and sounds of the film, your emotions are deeply impacted. You find yourself feeling tense, on edge and ready to scream.

Although none of what you're experiencing is true, it feels very real. You've been manipulated by a made-up story and some very good acting but at the end of the day, that's all it is.

If the influence of the mind on your emotions is so powerful in the span of a two-hour movie-watching experience, how much more powerful are the untrue, inaccurate and false thoughts that you consciously or unconsciously dwell upon every day?

Over time, false thinking unloads a perpetual assault on your emotions, to the extent that even your physical well-being and decision-making abilities become impaired. The Bible is relentless in its message that as believers in Christ, we are to replace old thoughts with new thoughts and false thoughts with true thoughts.

And here's the thing: many of us are believing lies that we are not even aware of. Over time, subtle half-truths, bad theology and false concepts of God, self and others cloud our ability to walk in the very freedom Jesus purchased for us. After all, "it is for freedom that Christ has set us free" (Gal. 5:1).

Do You Want to Be Healed?

As strange as the question may sound, Jesus asked this very thing to a man who had been physically disabled for nearly four decades. "Do you want to be healed?" (see John 5:6).

Why would the Son of God ask such a thing? Perhaps because, as odd as it may seem, some people have attached themselves to a sickened identity. They have given up the fight and have concluded that they are doomed to something less than God intended for their lives.

So the first thing to ask yourself is, "Do I really want to be healed and set free from the lies that assault my mind, will and emotions?" If you're sick and tired of settling for less than who God says you are and what He's promised to you through the gospel, we invite you to embark upon a powerful journey of deliverance and freedom.

Why only 35 Readings?

Because this journey is called *40 Days of Renewal*, you might be asking, "Why are there only 35 daily readings?" In our experience, we understand the fact that sometimes doing "devotions" can create an unintended sense of angst. While we encourage daily prayer, meditation and Bible reading, the sad reality is that sometimes we can become very legalistic about it, as though hammering through a few minutes of Bible-reading is somehow the point.

The point is never about how much ground we cover or whether we miss a day of formal, pre-planned time with God. The point is about getting to know and enjoy Jesus, the Savior and Lover of our souls. Sometimes we get busy and that "quiet-time" with God doesn't happen.

When we miss or forget or just happen to over-sleep, what happens then? Are we doomed for the day? Does that long line at the grocery store or that flat tire on our way to work become a signal that God is mad at us for standing Him up? As ridiculous as that may sound, there are sadly some who actually wrestle with thoughts not too far removed from that kind of mind-set.

Our hope is simple. We want to guide you through five quiet times per week with God over the next seven weeks. That means that if you miss a couple days a week, you're not behind! You can pick up the next day. It also gives you the option of coming back to a certain day or topic and spending extra time with God in an area that perhaps spoke to you with particular relevance.

This book is arranged in such a way that each day you have your quiet time, you'll discover one common lie that you will be encouraged to identify and replace with the truth from God's Word. The devotions are designed to be simple but not shallow, brief but not boring, and intimate but not intimidating.

As you meditate on each daily reading, we recommend the following:

-   Begin by inviting the Holy Spirit to open your mind to hearing His voice. Acknowledge your total dependence upon Him for the illumination and clarity you need to understand, apply and respond to each daily reading.

-   Ask yourself, "In what way(s) have I embraced the lie that is being exposed today?" Take some time to really think about this. It may or may not be clear to you immediately, but we have found that many people struggle on some level with each of these lies at some point in their lives.

- Try to commit as many of the daily verses to memory as you can. Scripture memorization is easier for some than for others, but do your best to memorize the daily verse and ask God to help you apply it throughout the day.

- Interact with others about the content if you can. Feel free to wrestle with things you may not initially agree with. Understand that we've intentionally avoided trying to answer every "Yeah, but..." and "What if..." that might arise from the topic at hand. We hope that this experience raises as many questions as it answers, so that you might develop the habit of being a truth-seeker and become a diligent student of God's truth through His Word.

- Finally, don't use this devotional as a one-time fix. We pray that it is a resource you can visit again and again in your spiritual journey. Some of the lies exposed and truths affirmed in this experience may hit your more strongly in one season of life than in another. Remember that although we have been made perfect in our spirit by grace, the renewal of our minds is a daily process that will not conclude until we arrive in heaven.

Thank you for embarking upon this journey! You are worth it! Jesus purchased your freedom 2000 years ago at the cross. It's time you begin to understand what that purchase means for you and begin walking in the freedom that is rightly yours by grace!

WEEK 1:

FAITH

Lie #1 – I must do my best and God's grace will make up the difference.

Truth: Life in Christ is a free gift from start to finish. While God cares deeply about the way we live and the choices we make, our performance has nothing to do with God's acceptance of us or His love for us. While man-made religions teach that we "give to God" in order to secure His blessings, only the message of Christ is uniquely and radically different. Man-made religion is law-oriented (i.e. doing leads to blessing). Christianity is grace-oriented (blessing leads to Spirit-empowered doing).

The New Testament teaches that "we love because He first loved us" (1 John 4:19). God is the Initiator and Giver in this relationship. We are the receivers and responders. Any measure of love we reflect back to God is from our receiving and responding to His immeasurable love for us.

This is such great news! Why? Because it means that we don't have to live under a "give to get" mindset with God. Our love for God flows from the gratefulness of knowing that He has already unconditionally blessed us with "every spiritual blessing in the heavenly places in Christ Jesus" (Eph. 1:3).

You can no more make yourself acceptable to God than you can jump over the Grand Canyon. The chasm was so wide that God determined He would stop at nothing to do one hundred percent of the work in rescuing you from that separation. God's grace doesn't "make up the difference." God's grace is the *entire* difference between separation from Him and relationship with Him. Rejoice in that today!

Daily Verse:
We love because he first loved us (1 John 4:19).

Daily Prayer:
Gracious Father, thank You that there is nothing I can do to make You love or accept me more or less than You do right now. Thank You that I don't have to go about my day subtly trying to earn or prove my worthiness. Instead I choose to rest confidently in the reality that Jesus has done all the work on my behalf to make me worthy. Rather than striving to do better in my own strength, help me to rest in Your arms of grace and allow my behaviors to reflect my gratefulness for Your unconditional love. In Jesus' Name, Amen.

Lie #2 – I don't pray / read my Bible / go to church / give of myself enough to expect God's blessings.

Truth: God's blessings are not contingent upon your commitment to Him, but upon His commitment to You. Again, this does not imply that your behavior is unimportant to Him. It surely is! But before we can truly walk in a manner worthy of our calling (Romans 12-16; Ephesians 4-6), we must first embrace how mind-blowingly amazing that calling really is (Romans 1-11; Ephesians 1-3)!

Christians do not pray, read the Bible, go to church, etc. in order to earn or secure God's blessings. We do those things in loving, Spirit-empowered response to the innumerable ways in which He has already blessed us.

In a healthy marriage, spouses don't go on dates, have late-night conversations or share intimate moments with each other because they feel like they *have to* or else their spouse will punish them somehow. Those connections are the result of responding to one another's loving initiatives.

As we discovered in our previous reading, God is the Initiator and we are the recipients and responders in this relationship. This is why in nearly every one of Paul's letters, he begins by laying out an understanding of God's amazing love, followed by an exhortation to respond with amazing gratitude.

Should you pray? Read your Bible? Go to church? Share your faith? Serve others? Yes! But what is your motivation? Are you afraid God won't bless you if you leave the house without going through some religious motions? Or is your communication with God based upon a guilt-free, joy-filled desire to know Him more intimately and experientially? That is what God desires for you!

Daily Verse:
Praise be to the God and Father of our Lord Jesus Christ, who has blessed us in the heavenly realms with every spiritual blessing in Christ (Ephesians 1:3).

Daily Prayer:
Jesus, I worship you in knowing that I don't have to "do religious things" in order to walk in the assurance of Your blessing. Every blessing is already mine in Christ. Instead, I thank You for the invitation into daily communication with You through prayer. I thank You for giving me Your Word to read and apply to my life that I might grow stronger in faith. And I thank You for my church family, with whom I can worship, give, serve and impact our community in greater ways than I could ever do alone. Please help me to recognize and give thanks for each blessing that comes across my path today. In Your Name, Amen.

Lie #3 – If I'm a Christian, that means I am a follower of Christ.

Truth: One thing many Christians misunderstand is the difference between a *believer* and a *disciple*. Both have a genuine relationship with Christ and equal access to God through Him. But only the disciple is actively growing in the relationship.

Among other places, Jesus made a distinction between believers and disciples in John 8:31-32 where we read:

> To the Jews *who had believed him,* Jesus said, "*If you hold to my teaching, you are really my disciples.* Then you will know the truth, and the truth will set you free."

In the Gospel of John, belief in Christ is synonymous with salvation. In this story, a number of Jews had embraced Jesus' message by faith (i.e. they "believed Him"). Yet, they now needed to understand what it would mean to follow Jesus by "holding to (His) teaching."

Jesus followed this encouragement with a promise that they would "know the truth" and "the truth will set (them) free." The word "know" in this passage refers to an experiential knowledge, not just an assimilation of facts. Jesus said that as we learn to "hold to His teaching," we would experience truth in such a way that it would set us free in every possible way.

If you have trusted in Christ as your only means of salvation, you are a believer with unlimited access to God. You are clean, pure, righteous and holy – but like the people of ancient Corinth, you now need to learn to "hold to Christ's teaching" in the same way that a baby needs to move from milk to solid food (1 Corinthians 3:1-3). Are you ready for that journey? It begins by renewing the mind with His truth (Romans 12:1-2).

Daily Verse:
Therefore, I urge you, brothers and sisters, in view of God's mercy, to offer your bodies as a living sacrifice, holy and pleasing to God—this is your true and proper worship. Do not conform to the pattern of this world, but be transformed by the renewing of your mind. Then you will be able to test and approve what God's will is—his good, pleasing and perfect will (Romans 12:1-2).

Daily Prayer:
Holy God, thank You that I can respond to Your mercies by offering you my mind and my body in worship today! May I be less conformed to the world's patterns today than I was yesterday, as I fill my mind with Your truth! In Christ's Name, Amen.

Lie #4 – If I'm going through a trial in life, God might be punishing me.

Truth: God does not punish His children for sin or any other reason. Because Jesus became the "propitiation" for our sin, He fully satisfied God's requirements for our sin in our place (1 John 2:2; 4:10). Through His New Covenant, God promises to remember our sins no more (Hebrews 10:17) and that His perfect love is intended to drive out any fear of punishment (1 John 4:18).

God does discipline His children, which is much different than punishment (Proverbs 3:12; Hebrews 12:5-6). Whereas punishment is punitive and born of wrath, discipline is corrective and born of love. Even responsible human parents will lovingly discipline their children to bring correction and the building of character. So too, we are to "endure hardship as discipline" (Hebrews 12:7) in knowing that God loves us so much that He will work "all things together for the good of (us) who love Him…" (Romans 8:28).

Persevering through trials is never fun, and is not usually something we accept easily. Sometimes trials are brought on by means of self-infliction, as the natural consequences of sinful or foolish choices take their course (i.e. "reaping what we sow"). Other hardships are simply the result of being hit with the collateral damage of living in a fallen world. This kind of trial happens through no real fault of our own. Some trials are even related to being persecuted for the sake of the gospel (2 Tim. 3:12), and God promises that through every trial, there are benefits to be found (Romans 5:1-5; 2 Corinthians 1:8-10; Phil. 1:12-14).

Whatever the case may be, we can rest assured that while God will use hardships to build character or bring correction, He is never punishing us. He never looks at us with vengeful motives or a punitive goal. His disposition toward us is full of love, grace and compassion, always and forever because Christ has fully satisfied His justice against sin!

Daily Verse:
There is no fear in love. But perfect love drives out fear, because fear has to do with punishment. The one who fears is not made perfect in love (1 John 4:18).

Daily Prayer:
Thank You Father for Your unconditional love and approval of me. Thank You that Your acceptance is not based upon my earning or deserving it, but simply upon Your grace toward me. I'm sorry for the ways I allow sin to gain a foothold in my life. I thank You that I'm not only forgiven, but empowered to walk in freedom from slavery to sin. Please help me understand that when trials come, You are not punishing me, but that You are gracious to use every hardship to bring character-development and correction where needed. Help me remember that "discipline" and "disciple" are related concepts. Help me to trust in Your goodness at all times, even when life seems unfair. In Christ's Name, Amen.

Lie #5 – God has blessed me so much that I owe Him a life of service.

Truth: While the above statement may sound true, accurate or even godly, it is deceptively incongruent with New Covenant life. There are many commands in the New Testament to live in surrender and service to God, but "owing" Him is never to be our motivation.

When Jesus died and rose again for us, He did so to *eliminate* our outstanding debt with God – not create a new one. Many people feel overwhelmed by God's goodness, and they respond by committing their lives to a sense of indebtedness. While those feelings may be understandable, they are not healthy or Biblical.

God calls us to live from a disposition of gratitude (Romans 12:1-2; Philippians 4:6; 1 Thessalonians 5:18) in response to His kindness (Romans 2:4), but never from a place of feeling as though we are somehow repaying Him. Living in "debt-repayment" mode will often lead to legalism and frustration before God. When we think this way, we will always be lamenting the insufficiency of our "life of service" in comparison to Christ's life of sacrifice.

These feelings of insufficiency will often plague us with an overwhelming sense of guilt and "distance" from God. Ironically, this is the precise opposite of what God has provided for us in Christ. Through Him we have been forever "brought near" (Ephesians 2:13) so that we can walk in the confidence of that nearness every day by faith. In contrast to living in "debt-repayment mode," living in perpetual gratitude will lead to a love-based motivation for serving Him (1 John 4:19).

It is because of God's radical grace for us that we can risk living lives of radical obedience to Him! Not because we "owe it to Him," but because we are so grateful for His kindness and we want the world to know! God wants to reach the world with the love of Christ *through you!* There is no doubt about it! But doing so out of a sense of obligation rather than grateful delight will eventually end in burnout, bitterness and bewilderment. Instead, live as God's ambassador because you are in awe of His love for you and not in order to try and "pay Him back." You'd never be able to do so in a million lifetimes anyway!

Daily Verse:
Rejoice always, pray continually, give thanks in all circumstances; for this is God's will for you in Christ Jesus (1 Thessalonians 5:16-18).

Daily Prayer:
Jesus, You paid a debt You didn't owe so that I wouldn't have to pay it myself. Thank You that my debt of sin has been fully and eternally settled through Your sacrifice. I want to serve You with my life, but cheerfully and willingly rather than from a sense of heavy obligation. You are not my slave-master, employer or debt-collector. Though You had every right to deal harshly with me, You have instead revealed yourself as my loving Father, my gentle Savior and my benevolent, holy King. May I walk in obedience to You in response to Your kindness toward me! In Your precious Name, Amen.

WEEK 2:

FAILURE

Lie #1 – I'm damaged goods...beyond God's redemption.

Truth: If you have breath in your lungs, God has a purpose and plan to make you into a testament of His redeeming grace. In the Bible, God is a God who gives "beauty for ashes" (Isaiah 61:3). The entire Biblical storyline is filled with characters whose lives would make most of us cringe with shame or blush with embarrassment. Some of the greatest heroes of our faith (think Abraham, Isaac, Jacob, Moses, Rahab, David, Solomon, Peter, Paul, etc.) had glaring records of sin and weakness, yet God still redeemed their souls and their lives.

After King David had committed adultery – and then had the woman's husband murdered to cover it up – David lived for an extended period of time with the ache of his deeds weighing upon his conscience. His secret guilt even took a physical toll (Psalm 32:3-4).

Yet, after David acknowledged a rebuke from an accountability partner named Nathan (2 Samuel 12:1-13), David came clean with God and received the forgiveness and restoration his mind and body were desperate for. David writes about these things in Psalm 32 and 51. And having come clean about his past, God restored a sense of confidence that he indeed had a ministry ahead of him. David said in Psalm 51:13-15,

> Restore to me the joy of your salvation and grant me a willing spirit, to sustain me. Then *I will teach transgressors your ways*, so that sinners will turn back to you. Deliver me from the guilt of bloodshed, O God, you who are God my Savior, and *my tongue will sing of your righteousness.*

Open my lips, Lord, and my mouth will declare your praise.

God never for one moment turned His back on David, yet David's secret sin made him feel distant. But when David came clean, God restored his ability to worship, serve and teach others about God's ways.

Daily Verse:
Blessed is the one whose transgressions are forgiven, whose sins are covered. Blessed is the one whose sin the Lord does not count against them and in whose spirit is no deceit (Psalm 32:1-2).

Daily Prayer:
Father, thank You for the total forgiveness You have given me through Christ. May I walk in transparency today rather than in secrecy. May my life become an open book, that shame may lose its grip and that I may walk with integrity. In Christ's Name, Amen.

Lie #2 – God will never use me after what I've done.

Truth: God specializes in redemption stories. You may have a rap sheet that you're not proud of. Perhaps you fear that even if God accepts you, nobody else would if they knew your secrets. None of that is true, of course. The Church of Jesus Christ exists to be a forgiving, gracious body of redemptive purpose in the lives of everyone, including those who have seemingly sinned "more greatly" than others.

Consider the Apostle Paul. Knowing full well what God's Law said about murder, Paul allowed his zealous interpretation of Jewish theology to propel him into supporting and participating in great acts of evil, including the taking of human lives as he sponsored and encouraged persecution against Christians. We don't know how many Christians were mistreated or killed at the hands of Paul and his posse, but we know that God took a man whose sins were far more shocking than the average person and turned him into the greatest evangelist in history.

Reflecting on his misdeeds prior to becoming a follower of Jesus, Paul said,

> For I am the least of the apostles and do not even deserve to be called an apostle, because I persecuted the church of God. But by the grace of God I am what I am, and his grace to me was not without effect. No, I worked harder than all of them—yet not I, but the grace of God that was with me. (1 Corinthians 15:9-10)

What are the sins that keep you bound up with feelings of unworthiness? Have you lied, cheated, stolen, murdered or in some other way been unfaithful? As with Paul, God has the power and grace to radically transform the trajectory and purpose of your entire life! Perhaps the question you must answer today is, "Whose testimony am I believing...my own testimony of my failure or my Savior's testimony of His redemptive love toward me?" Believe and receive that redemptive love today!

Daily Verse:
"Come now, let us settle the matter," says the Lord. "Though your sins are like scarlet, they shall be as white as snow; though they are red as crimson, they shall be like wool" (Isaiah 1:18).

Daily Prayer:
God of forgiveness, thank You for Your restoring grace. Thank You that even after all the sins I've committed and mistakes I've made, You have never once even considered giving up on me. Help me to take comfort in the reality of my ancient brother Paul's transformation, and make my life as much a redemption story as his. In Jesus' matchless Name, Amen.

Lie #3 – God is angry with me for what I've done.

Truth: The notion that God is angry with His people is as un-Christian of an idea as we can possibly entertain. Romans 3:25 and 1 John 2:2 proclaim one of the most stunning truths of Scripture. These verses tell us that Christ became an "atoning sacrifice" for our sins. The word "atoning sacrifice" is the deeply liberating word "propitiation," which was mentioned in day 4 of our readings.

Propitiation means that God's holy anger against sin as been completely satisfied through the sacrifice of Jesus Christ. One hundred percent of God's justice against your sin was fully paid for on the cross. Don't for one moment think that God is angry with you for any reason. God's satisfaction with you is the identical degree of satisfaction He has in Christ's work on the cross. That is God's irrevocable and perfect testimony, opinion and truth about you.

As His precious child, God's heart aches for you with the concern of a loving Father when you sin. He is not angry, but He does experience pain when His children act in ways that will produce hurtful earthly consequences for them and others God loves. He has given you a new nature and a new identity in Christ, and He longs for you to learn who you truly are as a new creation so that you will live in a way that accurately reflects your new self.

That journey is what learning to become a "disciple" of Jesus is all about. Jesus actually "became sin" for you so that He could receive the just punishment for not just your sin, but the sin of the entire world (John 1:29; 1 Timothy 4:10; 1 John 2:2). Because of Jesus, God's judgment is something you'll never have to fear. With this assurance guaranteed, you can begin living in a whole new way!

Because Jesus became your sin on the cross, you have now become righteousness in the sight of God. Because of Jesus' sacrifice for your sin, you are now as pure and righteous as Jesus is. You will not always *feel* that this is the case, but by faith you can choose to affirm that it is true! Rejoice in that today!

Daily Verse:
God made him who had no sin to be sin for us, so that in him we might become the righteousness of God (2 Corinthians 5:21).

Daily Prayer:
Heavenly Father, by faith I receive this truth that because of Jesus, Your wrath against sin is fully and eternally satisfied. Thank You that I can live with confidence that You are not angry with me. Help me to walk in that confidence in such a way that my lifestyle would consistently reflect Your character in increasing measure. I praise You that You have exchanged my sin for Christ's righteousness – and all of this is a free gift simply to be received through trusting that it is true. In Jesus' Name, Amen!

Lie #4 – My sin is no big deal.

Truth: One of the common and unfortunate misconceptions about God's amazing grace and forgiveness is that He is lenient toward sin. But God's grace does not imply Divine leniency. As we discovered in the previous segment, God's justice for sin was fully met in the sacrifice of Jesus dying in our place. The fact that Jesus absorbed the wages of sin on our behalf does not imply that sin is no big deal to God. In fact, it is just the opposite.

As we've already discovered, God hates sin precisely because it hurts those He loves so passionately (you and me). The wages of sin is death (Romans 6:23). Sin brings some form of death wherever it is allowed to run free. Death to hopes and dreams. Death to loving relationships. Death to possibilities and pursuits. Death to the peace of mind God wants us to enjoy in Him.

Though we ourselves will never experience eternal death, we *can* subject ourselves to the hellish earthly consequences of reaping what we sow when we live foolishly or carelessly. While no amount of sin can ever separate us from God, sin can and does do awful damage to the fullness of joy God wants us to experience through our new life with Him.

Through faith in Christ alone, we have instant peace *with* God (Romans 5:1). Yet our Heavenly Father also wants us to experience the peace *of* God in our daily lives. (Philippians 4:8-9). We experience this peace as we learn to walk by the Spirit rather than by the flesh (Galatians 5:16).

Is sin a big deal? Well, it was a big enough deal for the Son of God to suffer and die the most brutal death imaginable because of it. Let's rejoice in the freedom of our forgiveness, *and also* let's not get into the habit of abusing God's grace as a license to live selfishly or sinfully. We've been made new! Sin is no longer fitting for us and will never ultimately satisfy. But walking intimately with Jesus will! Do you trust that this is true today?

Daily Verse:
What shall we say, then? Shall we go on sinning so that grace may increase? By no means! We are those who have died to sin; how can we live in it any longer? (Romans 6:1-2).

Daily Prayer:
Father, thank You for casting my sin into the sea of forgetfulness and remembering it no more. Because I'm forgiven and new, I realize that my deepest desires have changed. Even though sin still seems alluring on the surface, my new self...my true self...wants the very things that You want. I yield myself to You as one who who has been made alive from the dead (Romans 6:13), and I choose this day to walk by the Spirit, resting in the finished work Jesus accomplished for me and desiring to bring glory to Your Name in the way that I love those who need to experience Your life expressed through me. In Jesus' Name, Amen!

Lie #5 – If I improve my behavior, I'll be worthy again.

Truth: It is easy to buy the lie – especially when we've recently blown it – that if we somehow make up for what we've done wrong, we will feel a renewed sense of confidence before God. This was one of the first human mistakes in the history of humanity.

When Adam and Eve first experienced the effects of sin, they felt ashamed before God and each other. The Bible says that they attempted to "make up" for their mistake by covering their shame with physical clothing they made for themselves out of fig leaves (Genesis 3:1-6). This was the very first recorded act of man-made religion.

Man-made religion is rooted in any human attempt to earn, merit or work one's way back into right standing with God. Jesus affirmed this through His story of the Prodigal Son, who offered to work off the sinful debt that his shameful choices had accrued (Luke 15:17-21). However, the boy's father (representative of God in this parable) would have none of it. Instead, the father embraces the son with unconditional love and approval, throwing him a party and celebrating their unbroken relationship (Luke 15:22-24).

Don't for one moment believe that there is anything you can "do" to make yourself worthy again in God's eyes. Your worthiness before God comes completely as a gift through faith in Christ (Ephesians 2:8-9). When you feel sorrow over sin, do not entertain the idea of making anything up to God. Jesus already did that for you.

Instead, confess your sin to God. This means that you "admit" or "agree with" God that what you did was sinful. Coupled with this humble confession, also agree with God that Jesus paid it all and that this sin was forgiven long ago on an old, rugged cross. Then rejoice that you have been set free from the domination of sin in your life (Romans 6:1-14), and begin consciously resting in His grace as Your source of both forgiveness and power to live differently.

Daily Verse:
He forgave us all our sins, having canceled the charge of our legal indebtedness, which stood against us and condemned us; he has taken it away, nailing it to the cross (Colossians 2:13b-14).

Daily Prayer:
Lord and Savior, I praise You that my worthiness is found wholly in You and no other. Thank You for doing everything necessary to present me blameless in the sight of God. May I walk in that blameless confidence today, in a manner worthy of the calling I have received from You by grace. In Your Name, Amen.

WEEK 3:
FAMILY

Lie #1 – I married the wrong person (Or I'm afraid I might...).

Truth: In a world that values the idea of hopping from relationship to relationship until you believe you've "found the right person," the God of Scripture puts the emphasis not on finding – but on *being* – the right kind of person in your marriage or any other relationship for that matter.

Think about that by taking it to its logical conclusion. If indeed you married the wrong person, that would mean that the person who was supposed to marry your spouse *also* married the wrong person, and where would that lead?

It would mean that the person who was supposed to marry the person who was supposed to marry your spouse has also married the wrong person. Which means that the person who was supposed to marry the person who was supposed to marry the person who was supposed to marry the person who was supposed to marry your spouse was the wrong person also!

If you just think about it rationally, is it accurate to believe that the entire human race married the wrong person because *you* married the wrong person? Here is a thought to humbly consider: Maybe you are *not* that powerful! Either we need billions of people to do a huge marital shift, or we can step back and admit, "Maybe we need to change our thinking when it comes this idea of finding the 'one-and-only'."

In fact, maybe...just maybe...this whole business about "finding" the right person has very little to do with "finding" the right person and instead has more to do with focusing on "becoming" the right person as a mate. Can you imagine how marriages would flourish if we changed our thinking here?

Daily Verse:
"Haven't you read," he replied, "that at the beginning the Creator 'made them male and female,' and said, 'For this reason a man will leave his father and mother and be united to his wife, and the two will become one flesh'? So they are no longer two, but one flesh. Therefore what God has joined together, let no one separate." (Matthew 19:4-5).

Daily Prayer:
God of creation, thank You for creating the bond of marriage and family. Regardless of my past or present struggles, I desire for my marriage and family to honor You. I am sorry for believing the world's lies about "finding" the right partner. Instead, by Your grace, I choose to focus on *being* the right partner. And I trust You with the results. In the Name of Jesus, Amen.

Lie #2 – My success as a parent depends upon how my kids turn out.

Truth: Everyone wants healthy, well-adjusted kids. For Christians, we also desire for them to love Jesus and walk with Him. While these desires are natural and commendable, they are not the determining factor for "success" as parents.

Both the Bible and daily life are filled with examples of people who came from great homes, yet ended up taking the wrong path. Likewise, there are many who grew up in terrible homes who, by God's grace, end up living amazing lives of redemptive purpose.

So how does God define success? As parents, our basic responsibility is faithfulness. This does not by any means imply perfection. Faithfulness simply means that we walk by faith in raising our children with love, discipline and training in the good news of Jesus Christ.

Will we do these things flawlessly? Of course not. Much of our parenting involves on the job training. As parents, we will make mistakes and plenty of them. However, we know that "love covers a multitude of sins" (1 Peter 4:8). When we mess up as parents (and we will), let's be quick to admit those mistakes and seek forgiveness from our children. Let's model a life of humility before them even as we maintain our God-given role of authority until they become adults.

And even if our kids are grown and we have unsettled regrets about their upbringing, it is never too late to seek forgiveness from our grown children for those things we believe need to be rectified. Ultimately, our children are free moral agents who are responsible for their own choices. They have their own will and make their own choices as people created in God's image (Genesis 1:26-27). They will make mistakes, and sometimes very costly ones. This is not necessarily a reflection on us as parents. If we are consistently humble and loving (and it is never too late to start living that way), we are evidencing the character of Christ in and through us.

Daily Verse:
Children are a heritage from the Lord... (Psalm 127:3a).

Daily Prayer:
Father, thank You for being my perfect Parent. I ask that my own parenting – whether now or someday in the future – would reflect to my children the kind of love You have for me and for them. May I accept the fact that I am prone to make mistakes in parenting, and may I entrust my children ultimately to You. In Your precious Name...Amen.

Lie #3 – Unconditional love means tolerating abuse from family.

Truth: While this statement may sound obviously wrong, it is amazing how many people actually live under such conditions, often for years on end. For a variety of unhealthy reasons, family members will tolerate significant disrespect, and even abuse, from those they love – all in the name of "unconditional love."

However, unconditional love in no way implies that we are obligated to tolerate blatant, unrepentant disrespect or abuse from spouses, children, parents, siblings or extended family. We are encouraged in Scripture to "speak the truth in love" (Ephesians 4:15), and sometimes telling the truth means confronting intolerable behaviors and having uncomfortable conversations.

Ignoring another's disrespect and abuse is far from a loving way to live. In fact, it is quite unloving to allow someone we claim to love to continue coping in unhealthy, angry or controlling ways. It does nothing to help them or their future, and it is quite an unloving way to treat ourselves as well.

Confrontation must always be done in humility and depending upon the severity of the issue, it may be wise to get counsel from someone unrelated to the issue who can help you think objectively about the best approach. Galatians 6:1 says,

> Brothers and sisters, if someone is caught in a sin, you who live by the Spirit should *restore that person gently*. But watch yourselves, or you also may be tempted.

Confrontation should be aimed at restoration and not condemnation. Though you may feel entitled to act vengefully toward someone who has wronged you, God exhorts us to "watch ourselves" so that we don't fall prey to the same abusive tendencies we're confronting in the other person.

Daily Verse:
"In your anger do not sin": Do not let the sun go down while you are still angry, and do not give the devil a foothold (Ephesians 4:26).

Daily Prayer:
God, You are the expert on relationships. You never treat me with abuse or disrespect. If there are people in my family who are treating me this way, please show me how to deal with the issue in a godly way. Give me the courage to reach out to someone for advice, if needed. May my attitude be restorative and not condemning. I am Your child, and though I do not deserve more than anyone else, I certainly *do* deserve to be treated with respect – and others deserve that from me. Help my family to heal in this area where needed. In Christ's Name, Amen.

Lie #4 – My family is more dysfunctional than average.

Truth: It is so easy to compare what we *do know* about our own situation with what we really *don't know* about somebody else's. These comparison games, while tempting, are unfair and usually untrue.

The fact of the matter is that because of human sin, *all* families experience dysfunction in multiplied dimensions. When a man and woman get married, they each bring some of the strengths and weaknesses of their respective families of origin into the creation of a brand new family.

With God's grace, we can learn to live wisely in seeking to reverse some of the most blatant dysfunctions, but there will always be family issues we fail to address, drama we'd rather not admit, and weakness we feel helpless to overcome.

One of the greatest things about being a part of the Body of Christ is that through honest, transparent relationships with other families and individuals, we can be reminded of how "normal" we really are. The manifestations of sin in our family may not look exactly like someone else's but the root issues are common to all of us: fear, anger, control, lust, greed, pride, etc.

How much strength could you draw from knowing that you and your family are more normal than you think? How much freedom might you find in realizing that you face the same basic issues as the people in your church and neighborhood? How much encouragement could you gain from pursuing transparent relationships with other Christian families through small groups and other opportunities to connect? That's what the family of God is all about.

Take the risk and get involved! There's nothing to be ashamed of. If someone condemns you for your honesty, that's a weakness in *them*, not in you.

Daily Verse:
And let us consider how we may spur one another on toward love and good deeds, not giving up meeting together, as some are in the habit of doing, but encouraging one another—and all the more as you see the Day approaching (Hebrews 10:24-25).

Daily Prayer:
Father, thanks for inviting me into Your big, dysfunctional family – the Church. May I have the courage to pursue honest, transparent relationships with others who will join me in the mutual endeavor to help each other grow. Whether I'm single or married, whether my family is small or large, we are all in the same boat – learning to trust You more every day. In Your mighty Name I pray...Amen.

Lie #5 – If I could change my family member, I would be happy.

Truth: One of the biggest lies we can believe is whenever we decide that our happiness depends upon the actions of others. Certainly it is never easy to watch our family members behave in ways that are selfish or destructive, but our joy in life does not have to be diminished by them.

Distraught married couples will often tell their pastor or counselor, "My spouse just doesn't make me happy." Frustrated parents will complain that the behaviors of their children are robbing them of joy. Why do we believe this?

Usually it is because somewhere along the way, we embraced the false notion that is the job description of our spouse, children, parents, etc., to make us happier people. But where do we get this idea? Not from the Bible.

In the testimony of Scripture, joy and happiness are to be rooted the unconditional grace and kindness that God has for us. The joy of the Lord is our strength (Nehemiah 8:10), not the behavior of other human beings.

Now, that's not to say that receiving love from a spouse, being proud of a child's accomplishments or sharing special moments with siblings will not add joy to our lives. Those things could and should add joy! However, when we look to others as the ultimate source of our happiness we are setting ourselves up for disappointment because only God loves us with a perfect, everlasting love.

We are never to put others in a role that is reserved for Christ alone as the "joy-giver" to our souls. We we do this we are setting ourselves and others up for eventual failure. Then like clockwork, we beat ourselves up and become angry at others because we expected the impossible from all parties involved.

One of the most freeing things we can do is stop trying to change our family members and instead pour that energy into loving them and praying for them in the midst of all of the weaknesses we see in them. Are you willing to trust God for the ability to do just that?

Daily Verse:
"Why do you look at the speck of sawdust in your brother's eye and pay no attention to the plank in your own eye? How can you say to your brother, 'Let me take the speck out of your eye,' when all the time there is a plank in your own eye?" (Matthew 7:3-4)

Daily Prayer:
God, I praise You for the family You've given me...blemishes and all. I realize that there is no perfect family, only a perfect Savior. May I choose to see the best in those You've given to me as my flesh and blood, as souls Your Son has died for. May I extend the very grace to them that I so long for others to extend to me. I ask You for this in Jesus' Name...Amen!

WEEK 4:

FRIENDS

Lie #1 – I deserve to have friends who won't let me down.

Truth: While solid friendships are a great blessing in life, it is easy for us to mistakenly believe that the performance of our friends will make us happy. As we discussed in the readings on family life, expecting ultimate satisfaction from human relationships is a huge mistake.

That is not to say that friendships are unimportant, but as with the marriage relationship discussed previously, solid friendships are built upon *being* a good friend rather than always *searching* for one.

Will you have some friends who let you down? Friends who commit to something and then back out at the last minute? Friends who seem to ignore you? Friends who seem unappreciative for what you do for them? More often than not, the answer is yes.

Often our disappointment with our friends is based upon the fact that we have unrealistic expectations. And although we should naturally avoid relationships with toxic people who tear us down, disrespect or abuse us, we must also embrace the reality that humans are deeply flawed creatures, which means that all relationships require risk on some level.

What kind of risk? Risk of disappointment. Risk of getting our feelings hurt. Risk of feeling like we're pouring in more than we're getting out. Risk of even full-blown rejection. Yet, such risk is worth it! Over the course of time, as we keep our eyes on Christ's power to *be* the right kind of friend to others, we can trust that God will supply us with some meaningful reciprocation from others who are focused on the same thing in their lives.

When our confidence is based on Christ's unconditional acceptance, we can love others freely without using them as a means of meeting our own real or perceived needs.

Daily Verse:
A man of many companions may come to ruin, but there is a friend who sticks closer than a brother (Proverbs 18:24 ESV).

Daily Prayer:
Heavenly Father, not only have You called me "child," but You have also called me Your "friend." Thank You for being the perfect Friend who never leaves or forsakes me. May I walk in that confidence today – and may that freedom propel me to be a true friend to those who need one. In Your Son's Name, Amen.

Lie #2 – I need more Christian friends in order to grow in my faith.

Truth: There is no question that Christian friendships *can and should* be a catalyst for growing in your faith. For the vast majority of today's believers, however, we often become so focused on hanging out with other Christians that we begin to lose touch with those who do not believe as we do.

Research shows that when someone becomes a new believer, that person will often be a catalyst for inviting their non-believing friends to explore faith in Christ. New Christians, though they may lack theological depth, are often some of the best evangelists because their entire scope of social influence involves those who do not yet believe.

Sadly, this wonderful influence in the lives of unbelievers often begins to change as people become comfortably assimilated into church life. We begin to replace our unbelieving friends with people who are in basic agreement with our faith. Rather than maintaining our influence in the world, we have created a "secular versus sacred" paradigm in which we must protect ourselves from sinful influences.

While Christian friendship is certainly essential, we must not lose sight of our mission to bring Jesus into these so-called "secular" environments. Do you honestly believe that Jesus has called you to spend the rest of your life doing Bible studies for your own "personal growth" while billions are unaware of Jesus?

What if a critical key to your own growth meant investing more purposefully into the lives of those who don't yet know Jesus instead of remaining only in a relational comfort-zone with fellow believers? Do you truly want to grow in your faith? Then take the risk of building relationships with those who don't yet believe! Don't feel overwhelmed. Start small – with your neighbors, co-workers, classmates, etc. – and trust God to open doors as you patiently love and look for opportunity to share.

Daily Verse:
Therefore go and make disciples of all nations, baptizing them in the name of the Father and of the Son and of the Holy Spirit, and teaching them to obey everything I have commanded you. And surely I am with you always, to the very end of the age (Matthew 28:19-20).

Daily Prayer:
Father, thank You for my church family and my Christian friends. They are essential, but they are not the only essential relationships in life. May I live more intentionally about loving and sharing Christ with others who don't yet know Him. May my life be filled with a passion for the spiritually lost. In Jesus' Name…Amen.

Lie #3 – I've been hurt so many times, I can't trust anyone.

Truth: As mentioned in a previous reading, relationships require risk. All human relationships will by definition run the risk of heartache and heartbreak. Yet, the alternative is far worse. When we retreat into seclusion in fear of the risk, we then risk finding ourselves in a place where we are not walking by faith.

Withdrawal from relational investment is a means of self-preservation that is almost always unhealthy. Our desire to control and avoid fear of rejection becomes more important than our call to proactively love others as Jesus has loved us (John 13:34-35). Our self-protective thoughts and behaviors can so easily hinder us from living on His mission of grace and truth to believers and yet-to-be believers alike.

Fear of rejection has induced an epidemic of social anxiety among millions. Our world encourages us to place undue emphasis on being self-conscious rather than others-conscious. Through education and media, we have it drilled into us that we are the center of the universe and our number one reason for existing is to be accepted by others.

This is not true! We have been accepted by the One who lovingly created us and whose opinion of us is ultimately the only one that counts! Nobody likes to get burned in a relationship. Rejection never feels good. But if we never face those fears or confront the possibility of being hurt, we lose out on countless other benefits of human relationships, including love, encouragement, and the opportunity to overcome the very things we're afraid of.

Perhaps you have suffered such significant rejection that it would be wise to seek professional or pastoral counseling to help you re-calibrate your perspective on life. Seeking counsel is a sign of strength and not weakness. But whatever you do, choose to resist the urge to allow past hurt and rejection to rob you of the hope of healthy future relationships. You are worth the risk!

Daily Verse:
So do not fear, for I am with you; do not be dismayed, for I am your God. I will strengthen you and help you; I will uphold you with my righteous right hand (Isaiah 41:10).

Daily Prayer:
Jesus, I worship You and thank You for your total acceptance of me. Because of that unconditional embrace, may I walk in the confidence that I do not have to fear the rejection of others. Even if the actions of others are hurtful to me, I do not want their actions to control me or rob me of the blessings of the healthy relationships I might discover if I choose not to withdraw. I am free from the control of others because of Your liberating love! I claim that now…In Your Name I pray, Amen.

Lie #4 – Church involvement is overrated.

Truth: We have already meditated upon the reality that we need more than just Christian friends. However, the importance of regular involvement in the body life of Christ's Church cannot be overstated.

The spiritual body of Christ's Church is described in Scripture using the metaphor of a physical body. Every part of the body needs the other parts to function in a healthy, productive way. The Apostle writes,

> The eye cannot say to the hand, "I don't need you!" And the head cannot say to the feet, "I don't need you!" (1 Corinthians 12:21).

The point is obvious. We all need each other in the Body of Christ. There are no lone-ranger Christians. Seeking a balance between relationships with believers and yet-to-be-believers means that a huge part of your life should be lived in the context of mutually drawing strength and encouragement from other Christians. You have gifts that others need to receive from. And they have gifts that you need to receive from. The environment of the corporate Body has always been God's plan for soul growth.

It is humbling to admit that we don't have every spiritual gift, and that we need to be on the receiving end of blessings from God through others. Some of the spiritual gifts mentioned in the Bible include mercy, leadership, speaking, teaching, helping, serving, generosity, encouraging, and a host of other qualities that God desires to display in and through His people. Are you willing to admit your need...and to minister also to the needs of others with what you have to offer?

Daily Verse:

For just as each of us has one body with many members, and these members do not all have the same function, so in Christ we, though many, form one body, and each member belongs to all the others (Romans 12:4-5).

Daily Prayer:

Savior and King, You are the Builder of Your body. Thank You for the opportunity to find true friendship with others who are a part of it with me. May I discover and use the gifts with which You've blessed me in order that I will become a blessing to others. I am blessed in order to be a blessing. I believe that with all my heart. May I put it into practice today, even in the smallest ways, for You said that a cup of cold water given in Your Name is significant in Your kingdom. In addition, may I be stretched to serve and love in sacrificial ways as well, and may I choose to obey when those opportunities arise. In Your Name, Amen!

Lie #5 – I cannot have a "best friend" without excluding others.

Truth: It is fundamentally not true that to have a best friend (or small group of best friends) automatically means you are excluding others. Jesus had twelve close friends that He chose as His disciples, and among those there were three – Peter, James and John – who became Jesus' best friends. Clearly, Jesus was not exclusionary toward anyone, yet He nurtured a circle of intimacy among only a few while He walked the earth physically.

What do we learn from Jesus in this? For one thing, we discover that because we are limited as humans, we do not have the emotional capacity to experience deep intimacy with everyone. If we think of our emotional capacity as similar to connectors on Legos, we can understand these limitations more clearly.

For example, a Lego brick with eight "connectors" can at most be directly connected to eight other Lego blocks. Additional Lego blocks can be added through extended connection, but they will not be as directly connected to the original Lego block due to the limitations of that block.

We can be genuinely friendly and loving toward all, but we cannot be best friends with everyone. Sometimes these boundaries even have to be set with people so that unrealistic expectations are not assumed, creating feelings of hurt and frustration and perceived exclusion. It is not sinful to admit your limitations. In fact, it is an evidence of humility.

So be careful to assess whether you *are* in fact being exclusionary through avoidance, dishonesty or phoniness toward another person. You are called to genuinely love those who God places in your path. But do not feel obligated to be best friends with everyone. If Jesus accepted those limitations, so should you!

Daily Verse:
Live in harmony with one another. Do not be proud, but be willing to associate with people of low position. Do not be conceited (Romans 12:16).

Daily Prayer:
Lord, I praise You for the close friend or friends that I have in my life. May I learn to be okay with my legitimate limitations. May I never use my limitations as an excuse to mistreat or ignore others, yet at the same time, may I view my friendships through a lens of humility and gratitude. May I focus on being the kind of friend that I desire in others. Thank You for being the perfect Friend. In Jesus' Name…Amen.

WEEK 5:

FOES

Lie #1 – I cannot forgive someone who shows no sorrow or remorse.

Truth: Because of sin, we live in a world of conflict. Forgiving those who have wronged us can feel next to impossible, especially when the offending party shows no remorse for the harm they caused. Still, Jesus commands us to love our enemies (Matthew 5:43-48; Luke 6:27-36). The Apostle Paul echoes the same (Romans 12:4-21).

Writing to a group of Jews and Gentiles who were frequently in conflict, Paul says,

> Be kind and compassionate to one another, forgiving each other, just as in Christ God forgave you (Ephesians 4:32).

How is it possible to forgive, and what does forgiveness mean, exactly? Many people confuse the idea of forgiveness with reconciliation, assuming they are the same thing or that the former always leads to the latter. But forgiveness and reconciliation are distinct.

While reconciliation is a two-way street, requiring humility and repentance from the offending party or parties, forgiveness is not dependent upon the offending party. The verb "to forgive" means "to let go of." When God commands us to forgive even our enemies, He is saying that we are to let go of the right to seek revenge against the person who wronged us. Through forgiveness, we are choosing to release the offender from punishment or retribution, even if we are confident such a response is warranted.

Again this does not necessarily mean that reconciliation will happen (although it could). Rather, forgiveness is as much for the victim as it is for the offender. When we forgive, we release the person to God and relieve ourselves of the stress of planning revenge and/or holding bitterness in our souls, which works against us living a happy and healthy life.

Daily Verse:
Bear with each other and forgive one another if any of you has a grievance against someone. Forgive as the Lord forgave you (Colossians 3:13).

Daily Prayer:
Forgiving Father, there are people in my life who have hurt me. There will continue to be people who offend, harm or attack me. I bring these specific hurts to You afresh and I commit, by Your grace, to release those people from my self-perceived right to walk in bitterness against them. Even if we never reconcile, I let go of the offense(s). May I remember this decision whenever I am tempted to fall back into holding bitterness. In Your gracious Name…Amen!

Lie #2 – My enemies are preventing peace and success in my life.

Truth: While it's certainly true that our enemies might come against us in ways that seem to harm us, like we've already discussed, we can choose not to allow other humans to have that kind of control over our emotions. We may not get to choose what happens to us all of the time, but we can always choose how we respond.

Refusing to allow our enemies to ruin us requires two God-given realities: perspective and attitude.

Proper perspective is found in allowing God's grace to be our filter through which we see both the blessings and challenges of life. If we truly believe that God is working in our best interest (Romans 8:28), then we can rest assured that when a door closes (even due to the attack of an enemy), our sovereign God is going to use the situation to bring about greater blessing eventually.

Attitude is when we allow a proper perspective to impact us on a deeply emotional level. In the case of our enemies, if God is for us (and He is), then who can really be against us (Romans 8:31)? We have been totally forgiven by God even though we never deserved it, so we can forgive others. The Savior who loved His enemies has filled us with His character, so we can love our enemies. The God who turned water into wine, multiplied bread and fish, and spoke all of creation into existence is watching out for us at every turn, and so we can rest in knowing that He will vindicate us in due time.

If you are discouraged, frustrated or angry because you feel like an enemy is destroying part of your life, choose to stop giving them that control over your perspective and attitude. Trust that Jesus will deal with the person(s) and focus your life around who God says you are. This is easier said than done, but you can do all things through Him who strengthens you (Philippians 4:13). Remember, the experiential peace of God is available to us no matter the situation or environment in which we find ourselves. It is not dependent upon the actions of others, but upon practicing what the Holy Spirit has taught us through the Scriptures.

Daily Verse:
A person's wisdom yields patience; it is to one's glory to overlook an offense (Proverbs 19:11).

Daily Prayer:
Jesus, I need to trust that You are my Defender and Advocate even when it seems I am being unjustly accused or attacked. Empowered by Your grace, I choose to refocus my perspective and attitude toward the whole situation. You are for me and not against me. You care for my every need. Even when emotions overwhelm me, I can do all things through You. I love You, and I trust You to empower me to walk through this with wisdom. In Your Name, Amen.

Lie #3 – If I could get rid of my enemies, I could finally have peace.

Truth: The Bible indicates that we face three primary enemies in this life: The world (Romans 12:2; James 4:4), the flesh (Romans 7:25; Galatians 5:13; 6:7-8), and the devil (Ephesians 6:11; 1 Peter 5:8). These enemies are part and parcel to living in a world corrupted by sin, and in various ways they will affect us until we are finally brought into the glory of Heaven.

However, just because these enemies exist does not imply that we need to fear them or be controlled by them. The *"world"* refers to the entire sphere of self-centered values that are championed as virtues by those whose spirits have not been made new by the Holy Spirit through faith in Christ. However, we have been given a new human spirit through God's New Covenant (Jeremiah 31:31-34; Ezekiel 36:24-28; 2 Corinthians 3:6), and therefore God has made us fully compatible with His ways and desires.

The *"flesh"* is that old web of habits and coping mechanisms that we once trained ourselves to live by when were living independently from God rather than dependently upon Him. The flesh is like old computer software running in the background of our lives. It is no longer compatible with our new "hardware" (our new human spirit), and yet it continues to try to draw us back into our old operating system of self-sufficiency instead of God-dependency.

The *"devil"* is a fallen angel whose name was Lucifer meaning "angel of light." (Isaiah 14:12). Lucifer rebelled against God and was cast out of heaven as a consequence of his fall (Isaiah 14:13-14; Ezekiel 28:12-15; 1 Timothy 3:6). He became the ruler of the dark forces on earth (John 12:31; 2 Corinthians 4:4; Ephesians 2:2) and is described as the accuser (Revelation 12:10), tempter (Matthew 4:3; 1 Thessalonians 3:5) and deceiver (Genesis 3; Revelation 20:3).

As children of God, we do not have to be controlled by sin through the temptations of these three enemies. As we grow in reliance upon Jesus, this objective freedom will increasingly become a subjective reality in our lives.

Daily Verse:
For sin shall no longer be your master, because you are not under the law, but under grace (Romans 6:14).

Daily Prayer:
God my Protector, I praise You that you have given me victory over the enemies of the world, the flesh and the devil. Please help me to trust in this objective reality even when my subjective experience tempts me to doubt that it is true. I am grateful that Christ's victory is my victory. In Jesus' Name, Amen!

Lie #4 – It seems like my enemies are from within my own family!!!

Truth: It can certainly seem that the above statement is true. As discussed in a previous reading, family dysfunction is a reality that every family knows all too well. In some cases this dysfunction can escalate into what seems like all-out war. What do we do when this happens? How do we respond?

The Bible teaches that ultimately, other human beings are not the real problem. Humans may be agents who are working on behalf of the world, the flesh or the devil (even when they don't know it), but ultimately, our battle is against spiritual forces and not physical ones (Ephesians 6:12). So what can we do when it seems that our enemies are the very family members God gave us (spouses, children, parents, relatives, etc.)?

1) TALK to God about it. Pray for wisdom and grace to direct your steps (Ephesians 6:18-20; Philippians 4:4-8)
2) TRUST God with it. Choose to believe God will answer your prayer for wisdom (James 1:5)
3) TRY to promote peace. As far as it depends on you, live at peace and leave their side of the equation up to God (Romans 12:17-19).
4) TEACH as many people who will listen to do the same. Be a humble force for solutions instead of pridefully contributing to the problems (Matthew 5:9).

Don't give in to the lie that other humans are the real problem. They may bear responsibility for pain they've caused, but ultimately they are deceived by dark spiritual forces at work. Through prayer and humble action, you can wage war against such spiritual forces and become stronger in your own faith as a result!

Daily Verse:
The weapons we fight with are not the weapons of the world. On the contrary, they have divine power to demolish strongholds (2 Corinthians 10:4).

Daily Prayer:
God of all creation, today by faith I appropriate the full spiritual armor You have provided as a free gift through Jesus my Conqueror. I trust in the belt of truth, the breastplate of righteousness, the gospel of peace, the shield of faith, the helmet of salvation, and the sword of the Spirit which is the word of God. Armed with these powerful weapons I stand calmly and confidently in Your unfailing love. Help me to see others according to reality, knowing that ultimately my battle is not against flesh and blood. Thank You that You have already defeated Satan through the cross and empty tomb. May I resist the devil's deceptions which seek to cause me to believe otherwise. I rest in Your finished work…Amen!

Lie #5 – I have no power to overcome what's been done to me.

Truth: Sometimes we feel like we're being held hostage to thoughts and emotions related to past trauma or disappointment. Maybe someone did something to us that we've never been able to share. Perhaps that person isn't even in our lives anymore, and yet the haunting memories of violation hold us in secrecy, fear, anxiety and depression.

The truth is that there is hope for healing from even the most heinous ways we've been victimized. Perhaps someone stole something significant from you. It could be that your physical or sexual well-being was compromised or disrespected. Maybe the weapons of your offender came through the power of their words.

Whatever the case, Jesus has freed you from the power of letting those things define you. Perhaps you need to talk with a professional or pastoral counselor – or even a close friend – about how to surrender to God those memories and feelings that haunt you. That's what the Body of Christ is here for!

As you learn to begin trusting in God's opinion of you while learning to reject the false labels that were applied to you through the sin of someone else, you can experience increased freedom from despairing and depressing thoughts. Replacing old thinking with new thinking and false thinking with true thinking, your mind can be restored and renewed to a place of mental and emotional health (Romans 12:2; Philippians 4:8).

You do not have to face this alone. Jesus purchased your healing with his own wounds (Isaiah 53:5). Don't settle for a life of victimhood. You are more than a conqueror through Him who loves you (Romans 8:35-39).

Daily Verse:
Finally, brothers and sisters, whatever is true, whatever is noble, whatever is right, whatever is pure, whatever is lovely, whatever is admirable—if anything is excellent or praiseworthy—think about such things (Philippians 4:8).

Daily Prayer:
God my Healer, I choose to stand in the courage of my Savior and pursue the healing that He purchased for me at the cross. I'm tired of allowing the sins of others to rob me of peace and steal my joy. If necessary, help me to identify the right friend, spiritual leader or counselor who can help me see through my pain from a more objective perspective. I choose healing over hatred, and I receive by faith Your power now to begin this journey…. In Jesus' Name, Amen!

WEEK 6:

FINANCES

Lie #1 – God doesn't need my money, so He doesn't really care how I manage it.

Truth: While it is certainly true that God doesn't need our money, it is also true that the way we manage our money is one of the most telling evidences of our values and priorities in life. Wise teachers have rightly stated, "Show me your checkbook register and I will show you what you truly value in life."

No matter what we say with our mouths, the money trail we leave is a far more accurate picture of the condition of our minds than our mouths ever will be. We live in an age of wastefulness and greed, and as Christians we are not immune to the pull of keeping up with the Jones's. CBSNews.com recently reported,

> The U.S. economy may be strengthening, but by one measure Americans are flunking the basics of personal finance. Credit card debt is ballooning, leaving American households with a net increase of $57.1 billion in new credit card debt in 2014... .

Keep in mind that this $57 billion annual debt increase is not related to homes or even auto loans. This is *consumer debt* characterized by living above our means and beyond our budgets. The "buy-now, pay-later" mind-set is indicative of how many average Americans are controlled by the false-gospel of "more."

Without shaming yourself in the process, take an honest look at how you manage your money. Are you living above your means? Are there a few gaping holes (or numerous small leaks) where your money is being drained into wastefulness? If you chose, by God's grace, to make it a priority, could you restructure your habits so that you would be able to save more for your future and invest more in the kingdom of God now? God doesn't need your money, but He wants your finances to reflect the priorities of your new identity as a citizen of His kingdom.

Daily Verse:
Let no debt remain outstanding, except the continuing debt to love one another, for whoever loves others has fulfilled the law (Romans 13:8).

Daily Prayer:
God my Provider, I admit that there are areas of irresponsibility in my financial management. I desire to honor You with everything, including my finances. I choose to make some changes – including seeking counsel if necessary – to begin gaining control of my finances so that they don't control me. In Your Name I pray…Amen.

Lie #2 – God requires that I tithe to Him financially.

Truth: While the idea of "tithing" (giving ten percent) is a common assumption among Christians, tithing was actually part of the Old Covenant mandates from which we have been set free by the New Covenant. While there is certainly nothing wrong with using ten percent as a basic benchmark for financial giving, the New Testament speaks of financial giving in different terms.

Paul used tithing as a foreshadowing example as to why vocational Christian workers should be supported financially. He wrote,

> Don't you realize that God told those working in his temple to take for their own needs some of the food brought there as gifts to him? And those who work at the altar of God get a share of the food that is brought by those offering it to the Lord. In the same way the Lord has given orders that those who preach the Gospel should be supported by those who accept it (1 Corinthians 9:13-14 TLB)

So while the New Testament never speaks *against* the idea of tithing, the emphasis is on generosity fueled by sacrificial love rather than upon meeting a legalistic requirement. While mandating ten percent is the typical line we hear in many churches, studies show that Evangelicals actually give only 2-3% of their income to the work of the Lord. How sad that law-based preaching, as usual, only generates a sub-par level of actual fruit from its participants!

Think about what could happen if God's people were to give generously rather than feel pressured into giving through manipulation and other human tactics? What if a thunderous response to God's amazing grace were the motivating factor in our giving patterns? What if this were true in your life?

Think about the single mom whose husband just abandoned her family. She wants to give, but feels terrible that she cannot possibly afford ten percent at this season of her life. Does God want her to live under such condemnation? On the opposite end, think about the many who could give far more than ten percent, but because they've been taught to "tithe" rather than give generously from the heart, they dutifully give ten percent as their obligatory religious routine. That's what legalism does. It produces condemnation for some and self-righteousness for others. Where are you along that spectrum?

Daily Verse:
...see that you also excel in this grace of giving (2 Corinthians 8:7).

Daily Prayer:
Gracious God, by grace I choose to give generously beginning today. In Jesus' Name, Amen.

Lie #3 – God doesn't care about the amount, only the heart behind it.

Truth: For those who are learning to live in freedom from the law-based demands of Old Testament tithing, it might be easy to surmise that God doesn't really care about the amount we give. Yet, this is also untrue.

In Luke 21:1-4 (see also Mark 12:41-44), Jesus commends a poor widow for dropping two coins into the temple offering, stating that she had given far more than the wealthy who were also bringing in large sums of money. While Jesus was definitely focusing on the heart behind the widow's offering, the amount she gave was also a primary feature in the story. Jesus marveled,

> Truly I say to you that this poor widow has put in more than all; for all these out of their abundance have put in offerings for God, but she out of her poverty put in all the livelihood that she had (Luke 21:3-4).

What did Jesus say? He said that the woman not only gave out of her poverty, but actually put in "all the livelihood she had." That's pretty incredible. I'm not sure that any of us would volunteer to drain our entire bank account, sell our belongings, and donate one hundred percent of it to the work of the kingdom, but that's what this lady did. Jesus' point was obvious: The woman gave generously and sacrificially while the wealthy folks gave minimally, even though they could have given far more.

In reality, God *does* care about the amount that we give. Paul marveled that the Macedonian churches gave generously, even though they were suffering from severe poverty (2 Corinthians 8:1-5). And He taught the Corinthians and Galatians about the importance of giving in *proportion* to the means that God has blessed us with, doing so in a planned, prayerful way (1 Corinthians 16:1-4).

Under the New Covenant of grace, the principle is simple: While the numeric amount or percentage may vary from person to person, God invites us to trust Him by giving generously, cheerfully and sacrificially. Are you obeying Him?

Daily Verse:
So let each one give as he purposes in his heart, not grudgingly or of necessity; for God loves a cheerful giver (2 Corinthians 9:7 NKJV).

Daily Prayer:
Generous God, through the gospel You have created in me a clean and generous heart like Yours. I long to be obedient to the impulses of generosity that exist deep within me, and yet I confess that often I often allow fear to prevent me from letting go of my finances. Help me obey! In Your Name. Amen!

Lie #4 – I can mature in my spiritual walk without giving financially.

Truth: Sometimes we might assume that if we are giving in *non-financial* ways to the work of God's kingdom (for example, giving of our time and talents), then there is no need to give financially. And while it is certainly true that we are called to give in non-monetary ways, Jesus and the Apostles clearly taught that there is a direct link between our hearts and our bank accounts. He said, "For where your treasure is, there your heart will be also" (Matthew 6:21).

In the context of that passage, Jesus is talking about not "storing up treasures on earth," which will ultimately waste away, but instead making it our priority to "store up treasures in heaven" where they cannot waste away. These earthly treasures include the material stuff of this life and the money required to attain it.

Money is not evil in and of itself. Like food, relationships, physical energy, intelligence, talents and other resources, money is a blessing – but it can be used wrongly or abused when turned into an idol. Paul said, "The love of money is a root of all kinds of evil" (1 Timothy 6:10). Again, it is not evil, but can easily become the root of many forms of sin, including pride, greed, arrogance, secrecy, dishonesty, etc.

Because of this direct link between our hearts and the money we have been called to manage, it *does* matter whether we are investing a portion of our monetary sustenance into the work of God through His Church. There are about 2000 verses in the Bible on the subject of handling money and financial generosity. Jesus spoke of money more than He talked about Heaven and Hell. Why would this be the case?

Evidently, God sees financial generosity as one of the most significant issues of walking with Him. When we are generous and sacrificial in our giving, we are stretched in our faith to depend upon God to meet every need. If you have not done so already, will you ask God to help you develop a plan to begin or strengthen this part of your life in Him?

Daily Verse:
For the love of money is a root of all kinds of evil. Some people, eager for money, have wandered from the faith and pierced themselves with many griefs (1 Timothy 6:10).

Daily Prayer:
God, You are identified in Scripture with the Hebrew term Jehovah-Jireh, which means, "the Lord will provide" (Genesis 22:14). I confess that I sometimes struggle to believe that, especially when my finances seem so tight. Help me to develop a plan to prioritize and give generously as a matter of joy and faith – and not because I feel manipulated by my insecurities. In Christ's Name...Amen!

Lie #5 – I don't have enough money to give generously.

Truth: As we've discovered already, generosity is a matter of the heart and not the size of our bank accounts. Data consistently shows that as a percentage of income, charitable giving among Americans actually drops as we become wealthier. And while we should never think of being generous as a means of "getting more from God" (as some Christians erroneously teach and believe), Jesus did say, "It is a greater blessing to give than to receive" (Acts 20:35).

The blessings of generosity are too numerous to list here, but the greatest blessing among them is that as we grow in joy of generosity, we are evidencing that we are becoming more like God in our character. We are developing a Biblical world view in which we are realizing that when we give, we are not really asking "What should I give to God?" Instead, we are realizing that because God owns everything – including the money He's allowed us to earn – the real question is, "How much should I keep for myself?"

As we mature in this world view shift, we become freer and freer from the grip of materialism and more and more excited to be partnering with the Holy Spirit in bringing the gospel to the world around us. There are poor people who are very generous (such as the widow at the temple discussed in a previous reading), and there are rich people who are very stingy. But how do we implement a plan to begin giving financially? Here are three essential encouragements:

1) PRAY – Begin by sincerely asking God for the joy and courage to begin making changes that will enable you to give sacrificially, whatever that

might mean in your circumstance.

2) PLAN – Obey God by developing a plan for whatever you may need to cut out of your budget in order to give to the advancement of His kingdom. If you don't make a plan, the sacrifice likely won't happen.

3) PORTION – As Paul said, "Set aside" that amount in a regular, disciplined way and begin investing that offering in the kingdom of God through supporting the local church as part of the greater Body of Christ.

Daily Verse:
Now about the collection for the Lord's people...on the first day of every week, each one of you should set aside a sum of money in keeping with your income... (1 Corinthians 16:1-2).

Daily Prayer:
Lord Jesus, my heart is in union with Yours. You have made me a generous person at the core of my new self. Help me to be obedient to that reality instead of entertaining the fear and selfishness of the flesh. You own it all! Amen!

WEEK 7:

FUTURE

Lie #1 – I've struggled so much in the past, so why have hope for the future?

Truth: One of the greatest lies of Satan we can believe is that because we have struggled in the past, our future is doomed for failure. We are tempted to worry about a thousand different things, including thoughts like:

1) My loved one suffered from illness, so what if that happens to me too?
2) My financial picture has been so messy, how will I ever get ahead?
3) That relationship was so painful, why hope for anything better next time?
4) I struggle with a repeated sin, so what's the use of believing I can change?
5) There is so much bad news in the world, why be optimistic?

The list of worries goes on and on if we let it. And yet, Jesus promised us that as we walk by faith in Him, we don't have to worry about the future:

> Therefore I tell you, do not worry about your life… Look at the birds of the air; they do not sow or reap or store away in barns, and yet your heavenly Father feeds them. Are you not much more valuable than they? …Can any one of you by worrying add a single hour to your life? …But seek first his kingdom and his righteousness, and all these things will be given to you as well…do not worry about tomorrow, for tomorrow will worry about itself (Matthew 6:25-34).

Jesus says that if God cares for even the tiniest sparrow in nature, He will certainly care for you as a part of His creation infinitely more valuable than a bird. What anxieties are you struggling with today? No matter what you've gone through, will you trust that God will never abandon you and will You trust Him for what seems like the impossible?

Daily Verse:
So do not worry, saying, 'What shall we eat?' or 'What shall we drink?' or 'What shall we wear?' For the pagans run after all these things, and your heavenly Father knows that you need them. But seek first his kingdom and his righteousness, and all these things will be given to you as well (Matthew 6:31-33).

Daily Prayer:
God of all grace, I confess that I struggle to trust You in all things. With my health, my finances, my relationships, my personal battles with sin, and a host of other things. Will You minister to my soul today, reminding me to trust You along the way and giving me Your peace that passes all understanding to guard my heart and mind in Christ Jesus? I am new! May my old thinking patterns be increasingly replaced with Your truth! In Jesus' Name....Amen.

Lie #2 – Struggling with fear means I am a weak Christian.

Truth: The lie behind this statement is the assumption that there are some Christians who are "strong" and others who are "weak." While some disciples may be stronger than others in specific areas, the Bible reveals that all of God's people – in both the Old and New Testaments – are weak in the flesh, but strong in the Spirit.

The weakness of your flesh is nothing peculiar to you. While various sins may manifest in different ways, our root struggles are common to all, including our fleshly tendency to worry rather than rest in faith. Paul wrote,

> No temptation has overtaken you except what is common to mankind. And God is faithful; he will not let you be tempted beyond what you can bear. But when you are tempted, he will also provide a way out so that you can endure it (1 Corinthians 10:13).

Not all fear is wrong or sinful, of course, God has given us the capacity to feel fear as a means of self-preservation. If we are walking in the woods and hear a growl, our sympathetic nervous system kicks in with a "fight or flight" instinct designed to protect us. Such examples of anxiety are normal and even helpful.

Unhelpful or sinful fear comes as a result of refusing to trust in God's sovereignty over one's life. There are indeed dangers in a fallen world, and believers are never promised exemption from all harm. However, as we learn to walk in the security of faith, hope and love (1 Corinthians 13:13), we can minimize the unnecessary pain of living foolishly, while facing the stuff we have no control over with greater confidence. If your anxiety is crippling in your life, you are no weaker than any other Christian, and you should feel free to seek the help of pastoral or professional counsel in learning to exchange that fear for faith.

Daily Verse:
So do not fear, for I am with you; do not be dismayed, for I am your God. I will strengthen you and help you; I will uphold you with my righteous right hand (Isaiah 41:10).

Daily Prayer:
Creator of heaven and earth, You knew the number of my days before any of them came to be and You knit me together in my mother's womb (Psalm 139:13-16). You promise that Your plans are to prosper and not to harm me (Jeremiah 29:11-13). Just as You have been faithful to Your people throughout the ages, You will be faithful to me this day and every day. May I trust You with those promises as You continue to renew my mind. In Jesus' Name...Amen!

Lie #3 – How can Jesus possibly be in control when the world is such a mess?

Truth: This world is beautiful, and yet it has definitely been scarred by the compounded affects of thousands of years of sin. In a day when we are overly exposed to bad news through technology and media, it can be easy to doubt that God really does have a plan in effect for all of this.

And yet, throughout history, the Bible reveals that God has broken in to provide healing and salvation in ways that seem like the eleventh hour. In His teaching on the end times, Jesus said to His disciples,

> You will hear of wars and rumors of wars, but see to it that you are not alarmed. Such things must happen, but the end is still to come. Nation will rise against nation, and kingdom against kingdom. There will be famines and earthquakes in various places. All these are the beginning of birth pains (Matthew 24:6-8).

In this passage Jesus even went on to teach His early disciples that they would face many trials, even including persecution and death. Yet Jesus goes on to say that these kinds of things will not continue on forever. The end will come at the appointed time, and when it does, it will be a glorious day as He appears for a second time from heaven to finally bring His full orb of salvation to the earth.

We might ask, "Why doesn't He come right now? How much more suffering can this planet take?" The Apostle Peter answers the question this way:

> The Lord is not slow in keeping his promise, as

some understand slowness. Instead he is patient with you, not wanting anyone to perish, but everyone to come to repentance.

Did you catch that? The reason Jesus hasn't returned yet is because God is patient with humanity and wants as many people as possible to hear and respond to the good news of His grace found in Christ!

Daily Verse:
He who testifies to these things says, "Yes, I am coming soon." Amen. Come, Lord Jesus. The grace of the Lord Jesus be with God's people. Amen. (Revelation 22:20-21).

Daily Prayer:
Lord Jesus, I trust that Your timing is perfect and that You have all things under Your sovereign control. May I walk in that confidence. In Your Name, Amen!

Lie #4 – We cannot know for certain our eternal future until we get there.… .

Truth: God has gone to the greatest possible lengths to ensure that His people can live with absolute security about their eternal destiny. Though false religions and even some Christian denominations have made the error of teaching the opposite, Scripture is crystal clear on the issue: Your eternal destiny is as secure as God is faithful to His promises. For today's reading, meditate upon the following affirmations of this powerful truth, with key ideas italicized for emphasis.

> I write these things to you who believe in the name of the Son of God *so that you may know that you have eternal life* (1 John 5:13).

> …being confident of this, that *he who began a good work in you will carry it on to completion* until the day of Christ Jesus (Philippians 1:6).

> Praise be to the God and Father of our Lord Jesus Christ! In his great mercy he has given us new birth into a living hope through the resurrection of Jesus Christ from the dead, and into *an inheritance that can never perish, spoil or fade—kept in heaven for you*, who through faith are *shielded by God's power until the coming of the salvation* that is ready to be revealed in the last time (1 Peter 1:3-5).

> Therefore, if anyone is in Christ, *he is a new creation*; the old has gone, the new has come (2 Corinthians 5:17)!

> …*if we are faithless, he will remain faithful*, for he cannot disown himself (2 Timothy 2:13).

And you also were included in Christ when you heard the word of truth, the gospel of your salvation. Having believed, *you were marked in him with a seal*, the promised Holy Spirit, who is a deposit *guaranteeing our inheritance until the redemption of those who are God's possession*— to the praise of his glory (Ephesians 1:13-14).

For I am convinced that neither death nor life, neither angels nor demons, neither the present nor the future, nor any powers, neither height nor depth, *nor anything else in all creation, will be able to separate us from the love of God that is in Christ Jesus our Lord* (Romans 8:38-39).

Daily Verse:
The Lord appeared to us in the past, saying: "I have loved you with an everlasting love; I have drawn you with unfailing kindness." (Jeremiah 31:3).

Daily Prayer:
Saving God, thank You for the assurance that You will never leave me or forsake me. Jesus not only died in my place, but He lived a faithful life in my place – and You have credited His perfect performance to me as a free gift, as though it were my very own! Your grace is sufficient for me, for Your power is made perfect in my weakness. Thank You that my eternal future is not resting in my feeble hands, but in Yours. I rest this day and every day in the confidence of Your unfailing love. In the Savior's Name, Amen.

Lie #5 – But I want to do such and such before Jesus comes back!

Truth: When we've been blessed as much as we have in this life, it is easy to think that, although we want Jesus to return someday, we hope it won't be until *after* we've seen or done certain things. This attitude is especially prevalent when we are young. "Jesus," we say, "I want You to come back, but not until...
  - I've graduated from high school."
  - I've landed my dream job or career."
  - I've gotten married and had children."
  - I've been able to see my grandchildren grow up."

The list goes on, and while such desires are not necessarily sinful or unreasonable, they reveal how little we actually understand about the future kingdom that Jesus will bring when He returns. The return of Jesus Christ is not an event for Christians to fear or be hesitant about. When Jesus ushers in the full force of His future kingdom, we will be transformed in a way that will cause us to wonder what we ever saw in the ordinary delights of life prior to His return.

Contrary to the cartoon-inspired versions of heaven, our eternal dwelling will not consist of disembodied spirits floating around on clouds while playing harps. The future heavenly kingdom will be as physical as our current experience, but will be perfect in every way, without any more tears, pain, suffering or evil (Revelation 21:1-5). These promises are for all who have had their sins forgiven by grace through faith in Jesus. For those who have rejected Jesus, they will sadly face a different destiny, not because God doesn't love them, but because they have rejected His grace found in Christ (Revelation 21:8).

If you have dreams and aspirations for this life prior to Christ's return, that is wonderful! That means that your life is tremendously blessed and you are filled with a faith-inspired hope that many in the world live without. However, don't for a moment think that if Jesus returns before you experience those things, you will feel somehow disappointed or like you're missing out. Nothing could be further from the truth!

Daily Verse:
He will wipe every tear from their eyes. There will be no more death or mourning or crying or pain, for the old order of things has passed away (Revelation 21:4).

Daily Prayer:
Returning King of Kings and Lord of Lords, I agree with the closing words of Revelation: "Even so, come quickly Lord Jesus!" Your plan is perfect – and if it is still a long way away, then so be it. But if it is today or tomorrow, I'm ready – and excited – to meet You face to face! In Your beautiful Name…Amen!

48913357R00057

Made in the USA
Lexington, KY
21 January 2016